Openings for Light to Pass Through

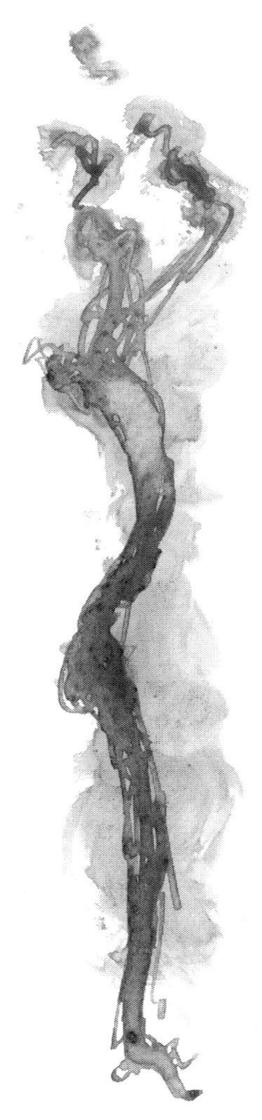

Openings for Light to Pass Through

Poems

Kimberly Cloutier Green

BAUHAN PUBLISHING ❦ PETERBOROUGH, NEW HAMPSHIRE ❦ 2025

ISBN: 978-087233-390-1

Library of Congress Cataloging-in-Publication Data:
Names: Green, Kimberly Cloutier, author.
Title: Openings for light to pass through : poems / Kimberly Cloutier Green.
Description: Peterborough, New Hampshire : Bauhan Publishing, 2025. |
Identifiers: LCCN 2025003881 (print) | LCCN 2025003882 (ebook) | ISBN 9780872333901 (paperback) | ISBN 9780872333918 (ebook)
Subjects: LCGFT: Poetry.
Classification: LCC PS3607.R43325 O64 2025 (print) | LCC PS3607.R43325 (ebook) | DDC 811/.6--dc23/eng/20250207
LC record available at https://lccn.loc.gov/2025003881
LC ebook record available at https://lccn.loc.gov/2025003882

Book design by Sarah Bauhan; typeset in Arno Pro and Electra
Cover design by Henry James
Printed by Versa Press
Cover image: wishes vs hope #2 by Judith Andrews www.judithandrews.squarespace.com

PO BOX 117 PETERBOROUGH NEW HAMPSHIRE 03458
603-567-4430
WWW.BAUHANPUBLISHING.COM
Follow us on Facebook and Instagram – @bauhanpub

MANUFACTURED IN THE UNITED STATES OF AMERICA

For my parents, Robert and Patricia, with great love
and for my granddaughter, Miri, with great hope

Acknowledgments

Grateful acknowledgement is made to the editors of the following journals where some of these poems first appeared, sometimes in earlier versions: *Mid-American Review, The Sow's Ear Poetry Review, The Maine Review, Lunation: A Good Fat Anthology, Hole in the Head Review,* and *New Orleans Review.*

Hawthornden Literary Retreat in Scotland gave me gifts of time, hospitality, solitude, and beauty. The residency is unique for its practice of day-long silence, supported by the absence of internet and cell service. For the peace and kindness I found there, I am so very grateful. I continue to feel blessed by every generous, hand-written letter (all saved and tied with a green ribbon) that I received from you, my dear family and friends, while I was away.

With thanks to editor Jody Hetherington for her careful eye and poet's heart, and to artist Judith Andrews for her graceful cover art.

My deepest gratitude, as always, to Douglas Green, the closest reader not only of my work but of my life.

Contents

Shefa

For life's inwoven
syntax and structure—
frame we move in
bone-hinge and hollow

field for each cell
city and star
for pattern of being
quanta and string

for the cradle and huppah
the crutch the stone
high banks of the river
and the river ongoing

love's spoken word too
its tune and bright thunder
for the circle of fifths
we say in the night

for sorrow we taste
sweet wetness and brine
and the darkness in us
You hover over

for this   more
there was evening, there was morning
I give thanks for the still unfolding

Orientation

Back then there were at least

three of me, each
on a different road
riding her own bike
in her own night
for scent on the wind
of honeysuckle, sweet
heat of the sneak
down streets overhung
with summer catalpas
all whoop and holler
joy replete
repeat, repeat
each white picket house
whizzing past as fast
as spoke-tick, tire-thrum
our legs out-flung
our arms out-flung
a racket, a ruckus
no pedals no bars
fat moon and star-throng
keeping up with our fun
and we the loudest that evening
alive, a tribe
unchecked and unkissed
and there was a perfect
freedom in this—

wild horse

before breaking, there was only
her being
in every direction

grass and cloud and hawk and rain

yellow suns   untethered
rose   dropped down

versions of herself
and as continuous

she couldn't imagine
bridle, rein
but sensed his sudden presence in the field
was not stillness

now everything even her hard-racing
heart is discrete

Artifacts that Might Be Maps

It matters who's at the wheel, where you're headed,
tires humming a low rumble on the road, hills rocking like the sides
of a great wooden cradle—let's say it's your dad up front,
his Old Spice aftershave and cup of black coffee
braiding with the warm summer winds that rush
through every open window—pine, asphalt, diesel, pine.
He's tuned in something classical, sad, that you hear
and don't hear, distant as that hawk gliding high overhead,
which you watch with one squinting eye, face tipped to the sun,
your hair streaming—even ranging like that, the hawk seems to know
exactly where it is, but if it's following signs, you can't see them.
Orientation's a mystery, a thing you'll look up when you get home,
whenever that is, and then you'll know how it works for a while,
sensors in the eyes—until the answer changes.
From the jut of his head you can tell your dad's thoughts
are strict, a knot, and the music, the cigarette,
his white knuckles on the wheel,
are a way you know it's hard, his life, and you can't help
except by keeping still, not asking *when will we get there*—
he's lonely, you think, maybe lost, another contingency
you leave for the road ahead.

In the Garden of Letters

In the garden of letters one figure's an ox
Another's a flood, now a shock of red birds

This letter's an axe and its lonely instruction
And that's a small cup for a shattering joy

Two over a wound and next a black thread
Amphora of oil, copper coin and a map

Close by there's a sea cow, no teeth in her maw
Her body unable to dive, and drifting

And that one's the wick in a lump of her fat
This other a season of grief and its hair

Here an acrobat fearless of falling
There a small boy and his hope of deep snow

See towards the back a boat and its rigging
Opium, walking stick, soup kitchen, kite

In the garden of letters you sense but can't see them
Ethereal bees, their hoard of gold light

Nightstand

In the lamp's cone
of soft light
the moth's sudden
stillness—
and the slow-wing scent
of mock orange, single stem
in a water glass

Two books at rest there—
in one, the mid-story girl is now
always now
slipping into the same cool pond
to float and dream—incidental to plot
some read right past

There are things you can say
in one language
you cannot say in another
so the books exchange
a violet breath

The words and the hushed
spaces between words
sigh and turn over in their sleep
forgetting all they meant

Tracking

A different course, you're saying, on our way to the hospital,
would be to stop here, climb that rock wall, hike into the woods beyond—
the blue tightness in your lips a sure sign of nausea
rising again as we wend along mountain roads in the early light—
last night's snow a perfect map for tracks, impressions like tiny campfires.

And when I wheel your slim weight into the familiar wing,
routine so numbing you lead comically, gesture broadly—
this way, now that—your pale arms conduct us down the blue halls
to a room only you can enter. You're still describing the trail we passed,
naming the trees, translating the runic marks we'd find and follow,
you out ahead, scouting—*like learning to read, clumps of hair, chews,*
scratches and scat, an alphabet of signs telling the life of a wild creature—
and I want to ask if a tracker can know and not understand what she sees,
but a nurse calls your name and the hazard door closes behind you.

In the time it takes me to heat water for tea, peel an orange,
you reappear shaken and straight in your chair, thanking the nurses,
touching their hands, then we're back in the car rearranging around you
the few things you've brought for the same road back—hat and towel,
cup and straw, amber vial of morphine and its black dropper.
You mostly doze. I'm glad for your rest, though the quiet's unnerving,
and the forests banking the road look flat without your brave narration.
Will what you've taught me stay—the animal traces of hunger, hiding,
direction and pace—how they somehow tell a story?
Or is the knowledge only useful until you come to a why like this.

Matins

Sometimes night
sky and dark ground
merge
and you're left
in *surround*—

what it's like   maybe
inside an egg

where you might tap
or listen

they're different
decisions

Ultrasound

Your unmistakable hands—
each translucent fingertip
a gas and dust star

and at the center of this nebula
your heartbeat—
one hundred forty beats per minute

Longed-for babe, little rivet,
you fasten us to the hurly-burly
dress all our devotions
in new rags

and with your sack of paste trinkets
you'll trundle your way
on the bone road we've paved for you
and veer off—drum-wonder
of your own necessity

I'm willing to believe
in repetition—each hitch we make
fire, flute, wheel and wing
to the carnival dark

Twinkle, twinkle
and live long past us— *See there!*
already reaching

Mother: Source & Slant

On waking I'd lost the word   just one
symbol you said in my dream
was the sum of our love
a single syllable root
beginning with *s*
like a key   a chrysalis
hinting at something hidden inside
and if I saw it I'd remember
so I searched the dictionary
pages and columns of *s*-words
little ones like *salt sap seed*
and knew you in their loyalty
blood and beginning
knew you too in *scent*
even now can close my eyes
and L'Heure Bleue perfumes the air
of a room you've just left
and here are *scant* and *scrap* and *sting*
which are measures
fragments and hurts
they apply   but feel stale or small
as *sea* is too large—*o you who pointed and named the sky*
who gave me my first store of words—which one
tells the whole story   *spy*
each of us keeping watch   like stars
from distances not fixed but constantly moving
or closer   quieter   not a word at all
but a whispered phoneme
kiss-shaped and breath-emptying
shhhhhhh
which means *hush*   and *listen*
let's not give ourselves away

all hosey upon them

she are running

and he are running

they onerun from the idols

tombspice and rollaway

their leg ache her breath pant

they notbeafraid

all achy like this

say the weshe who knows

the allalone one

mosttake a singular

run—

every girlboy raised

all hosey upon them

a cool grammatical

boneshoe we tied to

but eye place a new

where the old where the stone

eye place a homeword

the ithou and still

they running and running

we sure cracks our head
so brokehurt the falls
and the sky blackblue
still the heart where the old
and we're up off our knees
the allwish a painwash
of loss at the loss end
where the old where the stone
is ever a passthrough
they dreamsaw and run
and mostwise as one

Homing

— in the voices of women incarcerated at the Strafford County Jail

*

Who do you think you are, he asks,
unglued, unclued, his fix wholly rhetorical.
I'm an apple and I fall far,
a dreamer, a fever, a stray—
girl still settling into her skin,
all legs and the urge to run
toward a largeness I have no name for.

I'm a waif with holes in my pockets,
no bread, no honey to feed or appease you,
a wound, a wonder, and the slap that comes after,
the silence too, that sliver of blue,
when you ask who I think I am, I am
the one—you forget—who belongs to you.

*

Last light and the bird unpeeps.
New phase and the tide unneaps.
Neither here nor there, no clasp, no knot
every tie unlooped before it's not,
home's a slurry halftone,
unringing itself, outrunning itself,
past-wish bare as a bleached white bone
even a hungry dog lets go of.

*

Sometimes the quick's a cage and I count
linoleum paces, the blocks in the walls.
Hard to tell which eye's the ticking clock
which eye's the clock that stops.
Clink, clink of my chain. *Plink, plink* of the rain.

Letters come, I count them. Don't come, I count.
We have a pit in our stomach. It wants to be touched.
It wants to be whispered—it wants
the buzzing yellow lights turned out.
A guard watches all this. We look like sleep.
He places a wreath of wool for the dead.
My hair grows long and I tie it up, let it down, tie it up again.
I sit near the door. All doors are palaces.
They have chambers, *click*, gardens, *click,* and wings.

*

Once I saw bluebirds scissor down from the sky,
eight, ten of them, light in a tree. I held my breath.
Then they lifted as one and were gone.
What I recall is their verticality. Day with a blue bolt through it.
Pin in a hinge that binds *once and now, lost and found.*

*

Sometimes you knock a nest down, you can't help it,
the beak-bound grass and twigs, your own hair woven in,
all that effort, selection, and time, and you break the fragile cup
with its few tiny eggs, greenish-blue and flecked with black
that smash at your feet and make no sound

*

Homing, you know this, is finding your way back
by ear by scent by light by field, every hard-to-say word
a compass, a map, on thin-as-skin paper pinned to your sleeve.
It's knowing where home is and going to it.
But home's the thing you knew last by leaving.

*

Then the one I turned my back on sees me coming
and pulls the dog ragged and reeking from under the house,
where she's waited and waited for my return,
and she runs to me, that god runs to me, all mange and scar,
her eyes two moons in a cataract darkness, to press her warmth
into me, make us one flesh, lick all black gums and tongue
my hair my face my hands and feet
because I stink too, I stink through and through,
and this is at last a beginning—this dog,
this four-legged no-name mercy who walks me
the rest of the only way home.

How I Hold You

Stranger,

I keep this photograph of you
with a young girl draped like cloth in your arms,
her pale mouth slack, left ear torn away—
she was all you could hope to save
on that stunned and ruined street.

I clipped your image from the paper years ago,
but have forgotten what land, which war.
What shines outside the field of view—headlights? fire?—
makes bright pearls of your vigilant face, and hers.

Which grief first leads us to taste our tears?
Might she have done this—stuck out her small tongue
to lick her cheek, take comfort from the briny solace there?

In the picture a crescent moon and fierce little star
look like slit and hollow in a dark material,
chinks that well with a brilliance that burns
behind that ravaged night—a trick of the eye perhaps,
to see reflecting bodies as openings light could pour through.

That's how I hold you.

like sky

when he rolls over in his sleep
and lands
heavily on her
his weight so dense
and oddly   motive
she feels like something
in the way   a door
he is trying to open
she forgives him
dreams
are like that

anyway she's
awake now
could shimmy herself out
from under   but
she's curious

will a part of his brain
his inner ear
—something?—
sense her slim body   probably
not

the notion of being a door
amuses her
    okay   she's that
but beyond the door's
an element   clear   and blue
like sky

if he could just get
through

she's that too

Pear

It's a brown-bagger, my neighbor calls across the way
seeing me gaze at the single pear
that hangs from the smallest tree in my yard
and he means it will ripen more quickly
if I pick and store it in a paper sack

I thank him for the tip, he wants to be helpful
but picking the fruit before it's ready to fall
is not what I want

How to explain it's not hunger that stops me
but astonishment—the tree, only a sapling,
has produced this pear, just one, like a bell announcing—
life pouring itself out for more life

And now this sudden longing to see
not only its celadon skin—little planet, illumination, green ongoing—
but deeper in, where the stone-celled flesh is hard and cool
and farther then to the ovary wall
where the pips tucked into their tiny cups

contain the elegant code for roots, trunk, limb and white flower,
its need for light and grace of sweet rain—the urge it was
before it was named, and the secret this tree knows about bearing
her fruit—hers—to keep and let go

Choosing Hearts

In the dream she can choose which lung, which liver
from those that hang like dresses in her closet
—which kidney, colon—
more than one of each, so there's redundancy.
So like her, this hedging of bets.
Things do wear out—it's foolproof
choosing from two, so safe, like plenty of time.

Today she's choosing hearts. Identical, same maker,
but one's acquired a pajamas-all-day look and feel,
which is cozy, sure, but sluggish, full of denial.
Picking this one pretty much guarantees a surfeit
of TV, solitaire, chips. Hours at the window waiting for mail.
Asking nothing, it would thump its regular path
to the kitchen and couch, curl up with the cat
for an afternoon nap or tuck into that book (its title escapes her)
about the woman, red hair, who had only one heart
and it broke or she died, a sorry plot.

So she chooses the one that races a bit, zips long up the back and clings.
Tiny capacitor charms glitter in the sleeves, tiers of rose-colored silk
swish at the hem. *Plush,* she thinks, slipping it on, the tiny electrical
storms in its chambers bluely atmospheric. Not *ticker,* not *pump,*
more a dance, a tango—slow slow quick quick slow—all sway and dip.

This is the heart she glides out in, barefoot, the rain incidental,
streetlights like yellow chrysanthemums lustering the road.
Her feet make slapping sounds, a music contrapuntal
to the rhymes of this heart—*beat that turns its back on sorrow,*

jumps the track and sucks the marrow,
never mind the straight and narrow—

rhythm that stops at the corner diner
—even late it's open, steamy and loud—
one empty stool left, she'll make a new friend
and there's coffee and cake, spongy and tart,
like a wish, she whispers to the woman beside her
sliding the plate and fork for a taste, and their talk
until closing—*we've made it this far, our hearts are still choosing*—
is good company and time in lavish measure.

Return

The oaks make an arch above the creek road,
ache of russet light I drive through, think of you,
a few stray clouds, no birds in sight.

Forgive me, friend, the long summer silence,
all my good intentions—*write, write*—too slender, slack.

I'll make you uncomfortable with praise
but the poems you've sent—a largeness in them,
images like cracked husks, their inner meat tender—
my own hunger scrapes me down to the core.

I have nothing but scraps, dream-wrecks,
a pencil drawing and the ink one that came later
of the braided onions you left your last knock at my door—
we were headed for some rift, suffering a rift, or mending.

I try to imagine arriving after all these months,
the surprise in your eyes. You'll cover it well, glad for my visit,
but hesitate for the shyness between us, receive without fuss
the jam I bring, and in this way draw me in.

I don't know how to explain myself—melancholy? selfishness?
You are careful not to ask, trusting, perhaps, our history of love,
the silence that sometimes settles between us worthy.

Your poems, I try, and the onions you braided—
they marked a way back, not only to you.

Due Date

Waiting's a weirding
a mist a shroud
muddle of forest
hut and tower
fairyscape of bargains
starless and scheming

a fear, a fury so
gut-strung and sear
it gnaws in the brain
—let my daughter and her babe alone—
nightlong chant
like a rivet in the bone

God of crumbs
coins in my pocket
I've a hatchet strapped
to my leg are you listening?
Lead us away from the rat
river no last-minute riddles

Turn back the goat the wolf
the raven and bear
make the bridge safe the giant
slow and the ladder at last
too rickety—

in this story the children
are not yours, Terrifier,
they're mine

The Waking Room

You most mornings sought me out, rousing
and toddling to the kitchen in our old house
where I'd been writing, the lamp still on.
One continuous arc—your bed to my lap
and the stillness we made in those moments before
the day took off. I understood I was not to speak.
I was to hold you until my hold became something you
chose to break and words like *milk* or *cat* or *book*
emerged to shape what happened next.
I was to be an atmosphere, like this morning's winter
fog that settles gauzily in the trees, or last night's snow,
soft and loose, magnifying passages of unseen deer.
To sense where and whether I should step in
has always been a subtle instinct.
This morning you'll rise late, hot and flushed
with dreaming, a visitor now in a different house,
and I'll glimpse your child-face behind your drowsy woman's
yawn and stretch, your own baby daughter reaching
out for you from my lap. I do not tell you what I've seen,
vivid memory belonging only to me.
There was a clock in that old waking room, and sometimes
its ticking was all that broke our morning quiet.

An Unfinished Story

She has slipped off her shoes
and climbed the stone steps
to the dogwoods overhanging the yard,
where she sits now to cool
her feet in the grass—
close by, her child listens to birds.
His absorption, briefest hush,
is a kind of absence.

He has always been fastidious—that neatness
in his small weight, his close attentions, quick
pulse in the blue vein at his temple—
asking again and again not only the name
but the life of every bird.

She keeps an unfinished story in each
pocket of her heart—longing
for everything, for nothing, for radiance
is every tale's beginning.

Her body is a river he'll cross
on a bridge the birds shape with their wings.
Impossible for light to stand still, she thinks
seeing him wave from the far bank.

Meanwhile the trees in the yard
pour down their green shine.
Wood thrush, she says, *omnivorous*
as listening he strokes
the rough bottoms of her feet.

Cataract

You left and I became a waterfall—
the cataract and precipice too

Some it's true climbed up through me
thrilling at my hard descent, thundering rush
of terracing streams

Near the high ledge, one touched too close
the pressure in my throat

I almost spoke

It's not what you think—
I didn't weep

I poured myself out, bright fan over the cliff face
glittering tiers flush with what breaks and breaks
down the mineral-scented years in my veins

I wanted more than seasons, lifetimes

Body in a Blue Field

This figure has let slip her silk robe, but her near
nakedness is incidental—
rapt in blue light her luminous gaze
hints at a lavish attention, she

is a blue body in a blue field,
and the field is every blue—cornflower, cerulean—
shades that drift in slow waves through her mind
and scatter—a color is never seen as it truly is
and this is some of her pleasure, the rest

is that it touches her, this light, the way his brush traces
—without haste, trembling, almost not touching—
her face, her throat and breasts
the blue length of her thigh—how hard he tries
to capture—not sapphire, not lapis—a sky
interior to her, a radiance her body draws its shape from,
like timbre or mood, more sensed than seen,
every fleck only partly true—

Close your eyes, she thinks but doesn't say,
to feel how they stream, the myriad hues
—given, extravagant—
through every boundary of body and field,
deepen, disperse, across infinite space, appear, disappear, reappear
now azure, now indigo, here and here and here

Playing Stick

He's all urgent eye and torqued joy
willing to play at this small obedience—*sit*—
bit of theater her round of stick
opens with. This dog's no wink-wink hipster,
no cheeky seen-it-all ironist, laughing at the joke
and then at everyone who doesn't get it.
This game's infinite, sincere, beginning
in attention, his eye on the stick—no winners, losers—
just this momentary wait for the toss and run.
She waves it in the air like a wand, wag of magic,
but the mesmer's not in the stick—it's her word, *fetch,*
which in Dog Etymology means *find your way, bring back* and *marry,*
as in *make a golden ring of away and return*—and there it is!
Her wind-up, stride and whip—and the stick's in the air,
slicing through all that blue ether along an arc he knows
without once looking up, and she marvels at this,
his genius, the law of falling bodies inborn—and see
how he dashes to the drop and he's never far off?
O homeless soul! A cry she doesn't utter but for a split second
shudders through her, until he turns all slobbery flews and whiskers
back for her, some ancient wolfish gene remembering survival,
how cold it was before they made a wedding of it.

Reunion

Do you want to see my scars? she asks, elbows up and out like wings, her white tee bunched in fists at her chin. We are sitting among the fruit trees in her yard, the glaring sun scissoring through, a host of wind-spinning cherry petals falling around us. She's talking, talking, the way she always talks—diagnosis, chemotherapy, radiation—fast, no stops, *and anyway my breasts were too large, too heavy, I'm glad not to carry that weight, the come-ons and whistles, now those who don't know me can't tell if I'm female, male, my bald head and flat chest confusing. As girls—remember?—we shimmied all summer like snakes on our bellies, no breasts, no hips, just the long cool rub of grass and its stains. I've got it back, that body.* She's brave, yes, but the still-red slits, tied with black thread, look like eyes shut tight against fear. *I used to think I could make myself invisible. Did you?*

High Fidelity

You have lived forty years or more
and suddenly you cry and cry
you can't stop crying, your hands clenching
the wheel and the road a blur

Not because your father's gone,
your mother too—you'd give
anything to see them
as they were once
happy-eyed, a little drunk
mugging for the camera

And not for the girl on the radio
singing an old song, high and clear—
they taught you these melodies,
harmony in thirds—

but because what you've never heard before
aches more—each barely audible inhale,
catch or click in the throat,
breaks we brave our way through
when we know what we can and cannot hold

It Could Turn to Me. It Could Turn Me.
I Could Turn Away.

It Could Turn to Me. It Could Turn Me. I Could Turn Away.

I am following a great fish
that emerges and disappears
in a blue and amber river   I am poling my way
on a wooden raft   the day-drenching
honeylight on watersilk
a near distraction   but I fix
on the fish
glimpsed only as parts   blackflash gleam
of fin or tail
onyx glyphs   half-circles   lines
repeating signs   broad head and spine
that slip the sun-dazzled
membrane between us
to dive and rise *alive alive*
and lengthen again in an undulant glide
streams of low-chiming
bells in its wake   It senses
the effort I make in relation
my distance   kept as time
skimming the veil
as though I were a likeness   shadow
or we are the way of everything watchful
cloud mud leaf bird flow
who keep faith with the river   one
breathing

Otherworlding

The path to the quarry is narrow

bone-white, the August heat a wall

of grasshopper chirr we press through, you out ahead of me

loping for water   stone-deep, cold   black mirror

ringed by pines and riffled by coppery tracings

of breezes that loop and race—so startling

your sudden sprint and thrust off a high rock   the long arc

of your scissoring dive a nearly splashless slip inside the skin of this lake

I watch your magnified form

undulate   roll like an otter   lungs full of summer

then see it split into light-crazed facets and cubist planes   shoaling fractals

that surge and sway and finally fade when I lose

sight of you in the darkness that deepens farther out

otherworlding you call it

all spine   heartbeat   strange, even to yourself

in the underwater life and rot where even joy is strange

Why do I hang back?   not cold   pressure in my ears

the tissue-soft mud and its throng   but my nature

to slow at the edge   keep a mild distance   let the world slip itself

into me—*wind trace   bird flash   your wholeness fractured by angles of light*

o the pleasure of being filled like that!

to enter the threshold between rock and water   is length and breadth

of a wildness in which would I lose myself—not flying or falling

but emptying   a pocket turned inside out

—your upsprung lunge and lift at the far bank

is a single bound out of water   one continuous stroke

rib bellows heave-breathing the sudden air

water sheathing from your height and heft   *Dive!*

you call from the reach between us   *Dive!*

and I do

Jet Lag

For days I'm black lines on white paper, circle for a head,
dashes for the body, arms and legs akimbo, no hatching for depth,
light or shadow, all shuck. Or the cutout figure in an alien
landscape collage, clown fish searching for algae in an alpine
valley's ash and scree. I'm hard to remember in limbo,
woman making her own acquaintance, easily startled,
terrified she'll lose her phone and wallet, passport and keys.
I pat my pockets for them as though they're talismans promising
every trail's a loop, but wonder whether what I've left behind
is the truest thing about me. Everything in this fog is subject to revision.
I scuttle my way forward through the unfamiliar city,
like a scarab pushing her tiny golden sun.

Intruder

When I first came upon her on my evening walk
I didn't know what I was looking at—
sack in the road? something fallen from a truck?
It took a moment to see her black heft, still as rock,
was a creature alive, staring dully at me, her tapered muzzle
and narrow shoulders glassy in the bluish light
of a buzzing streetlamp. I marked the distance between us,
the houses on either side, and didn't move.
She seemed—*what?*—disinterested.
As though she'd sniffed out what she needed long before
I entered the scene—not food, plentiful here, spilling out of
garbage cans. I could cut through a neighbor's yard
and return that way, but waited at the edge of the measure
between us, wondering if she'd move and in which direction.
Where could she hide in this neighborhood of skimpy pines
and checkerboard lawns? Sorrow then, not fear, rose up in me
for the secret life my turn away would not restore
and I made my trespass home.

Riddle

I began as impression
shallow basin
for what in time
poured into me
deep-gullying rush and ice-bite
both kinds of touch
scoop and hollow
for deeper fullness—
then a surge of years
skidded past

Below my wind-riffled surface
grew chara, wild celery
long-necked lilies
necklaced in oxygen strings
and farther down in darkness
the mud-tucked eggs

Your face came later
hovering
seeing and not seeing
I spied the smallest
version of myself
in your eye—*thing*
—lake, mirror—

Who are you, brother, who fishes
and fishes for more, sure
every silver flash in me is yours

Hon

I'm being punished and watching myself
being punished, in pain and watching pain,
in a room made of cinderblocks, all gray.
See how easily I turn toward my jailer,
how limp I am, as he, tying me to a chair,
threads chains around my wrists and shoulders,
and locks into place the thing he calls The Gate.
He makes his *yuk yuk yuk* sound.

I don't know what I've done wrong but no one's
innocent. I close my eyes and see there's a way
I've split myself—one part in pain, one part calm,
survival needing division. *People are many things,*
says my jailer, waxing philosophical, calling me *hon*
and patting his pockets for a pack of smokes.

Even now, when it's morning and birds are filling themselves
fat at the feeder, dream scraps in dark patches stay.
I reach for what fragments elude me—wanting to know
and not wanting to know how I ever got out of that room.

Because there was that last part, remaining shred,
where I'm searching the halls and the jailer's my friend
and we're finding our way out together.
Someone came for us. *Who came for us?*
The locks on the door to that cell were broken,
smashed from the outside, and I still feel each swing,
each blow—the force it took to release us—in my arms,
or in the arms of the one who saved us.

After the storm

a ghost-storm stays, light swallower,
the way to the beach strewn here and there
with weaker limbs, crow-squall and generator-din
no match for the wind, heave and whip
of waves against the highest berms.

Last night I was one of those glass fish that live
in the midnight zone, blind, scoop-mouthed,
hungry for anything that filters from above, my being felt
not as pulse but pressure, more water than bone—
were I to die, no weight would be lost.

There was more but I can't recall the rest,
except how vast and still the black
depths of that sea, how fragile that body—
no words for the thing pressing down and down
even as this time it passed over.

Hawk, Crab

Not only the startled hawk
rocketing, reeling
up from the wind-whipped water

but also the crab, all white,
large as the bird
and tied to the raptor's body
so tightly they rise
in a whirling blur of beak and claw
carapace, feather

a single winged and suffering body
that swerves, jerks, suddenly dives down
then thrusts itself skyward again

equal cravings bound in knots
of sea wrack and rope
each straining for its opposite element

entanglement even I can feel
watching alone on the old town pier
and pointing, shouting, flapping my arms
at terror in every direction

Claim

The wind of course, whipping against the house, rattling the glass,
the cold all night seeping in. Now it grazes my ankles
as I move about the kitchen, or feel it, ice-ghost,
when I reach inside the drawer for a spoon, not trapped
so much as keeping to itself, crouching there and biding its time.

Another well of cold in the cabinet, pocket in the box of tea,
even the bag's a small purse of cold—and as I fill a pot with water,
put it on to boil, I feel the chill slip up the insides of my arms,
circle the back of my neck, exhale of last night's starlessness
and snow-flocked pines on my skin.

In the closet a column of cold, the creek and its rime-covered rocks.
I sniff at it like a hound, nose in the air, try to pick up the scent
of what's trespassed, but feel it withdraw when I do, or disperse.
It knows this old house better—every thin place, crack, bit of rot—
can come and go as it pleases through apertures unknown to me,

and has, and will.
I search for more, open other cupboards, other drawers,
feel the insides of cups, shoes, books, reach down behind my desk
to find there, as everywhere, the cold has tucked—not stolen—in,
as though pausing, a quiet and patient thing.

I try each time to touch what's there as if it were material—
not only the cold but the night it came in on, waning moon and fox,
birch and horned owl, this frigid winter and the ones before,
the years, ages, millennia, land bridge and steppe—touch all the way in
to where I know it reaches for me, and my every small belonging.

Paper Figure Descending, Animated Still

—inspired by the work of artist Hanne Frey Huso

Handmade of beaten silk, hemp and paste
this lint-like figure—no armature, hinge—
does not grip but grazes
the railing of a black stair

Behind her, backlit kozo paper
makes a dusky atmosphere
flecked with marks like miniature wings
or slipper-shaped paramecia

One arched foot, just stepping down,
seems coy, even vain
but she keeps an aquiline attention
on her descent—*I want*

the place where I am buried
to be as beautiful—with openings
for light to pass through

Valentine

You must have read my mind
dear wound-dresser
dear *a-child-could-have-made-it—*
two cut-out hearts, made from a scrap
of cotton gauze, airy material
and laid upon a white paper field
one atrial curve just touching the other—

must have known I'd blow one soft breath
to see the unfixed image slip from its page
lift against gravity and briefly glide
then fall in the wordless and everywhere light
where these meant-to-be-dismantled
hearts began—

Make me something I can't hold—no ink, no glue—
make me something true

Malakh

She's not ungrateful, death isn't empty—
there's the faint scent of thyme,
a meadowlark's tune disembodied, yes,
but unmistakable.
She understands these are gifts,
a shining that pours itself into her
as scent and song.

And she means to be faithful
but her heart, it feels like a heart,
is big and mute
and she from time to time
forgets her place, though she's free to go,
message or no—
the heavens (they aren't called that)
don't fasten.

She can slip through that radiant physics
as though she were string. It doesn't hurt.
Visiting's like the stones she gathers,
wish-heavy and secreted in her pockets.
It's true she could cling
and she tries not to cling—

but her weight, its gravity, is a deep pleasure,
exquisite strain to move her limbs
or lift her head—and the pasture, green and wet
and bound on all sides by fences,
inhales   exhales   like an animal beneath her.

She has never, not once, turned her back on wonder—
even now she lies face to the sky
and ponders what it's thinking.

But from her distance, words come—
necessary, exact, an ache in her throat,
lines for little bluestem, timothy and rye,
for birds and rain and worms and bees.
For the body of the world, how everything breathes.

Notes

For several years I had the good fortune to facilitate a writing workshop with women writers at the Strafford County Jail. I have always believed that people are many things, and my experience of the women I met during this time deepened my appreciation of the many selves that live in us, the truest of them striving to step forward and be known. It is my sincere hope that my poem "Homing" (pg. 28) gives honor and blessing to the women who inspired it.

Some of the poems in this collection were written during the pandemic. "Choosing Hearts" (pg. 36) is inspired by a dream I had during that time. I felt moved back then by the collective sharing of dreams, so many people trying to integrate the frightening and lonely shutdown days in this way. "Shefa", too, is a poem I wrote during this period. Shefa is the Hebrew word for *flow, abundance.*

"Body in a Blue Field" (pg. 43) was inspired by a pastel painting by the artist Judy Bryant. The figure has stayed with me for years, and the poem has been through many versions as I've tried to imagine my way into the interior life of the woman in the painting. Joseph Albers's *Interaction of Color*, Wassily Kandinsky's *Concerning the Spiritual in Art,* and Siri Hustvedt's essay collection, *A Woman Looking at Men Looking at Women,* are just three of the books that have helped me approach the predicament that is at the heart of this poem.

My poem "Paper Figure Descending, Animated Still"(pg. 59), refers to the silk-fiber figure of a woman descending a staircase—a still from the animated film *Hornfels,* 2015, created by the hand papermaking artist Hanne Frey Huso. I understood the figure to have a kind of correspondence with my own time of life. In her poetry collection, *Come and See* (Graywolf, 2011), the poet Fanny Howe writes: "The image is a representation of a secret self, the being one longs to be, the self one never was in history, but remembers."

The three Abrahamic religions have conceived of hierarchies of angels. There's enough material there for a lifetime of head-scratching, if not art-making. I discovered this while I was reading Carlo Rovelli's *Seven Brief Lessons on Physics* and Feynman's lectures on quantum mechanics. More head-scratching. My poem "Malakh" (pg. 61) emerged out of all this. In Judaism, the Malakhim are among the lowliest angels, those closest to the Earth.